Gigi's Golden Garden

Written by Emilee Powell

Illustrated by Bannarot S.

This book is dedicated to my amazing grandparents who embody strength, faithfulness, generosity, and unconditional love.

A huge thank you to my amazing Kickstarter supporters that helped bring this book to life—especially the gold tier supporters:

Gerald and Carylyn Pippenger

Glenda Guthrie

Eric Powell

Larry and Robbie Butts

Chimene and Dave Tingue

At the back of the book, you will find a discussion section that includes the Biblical context from the story.

I hope you enjoy this special story of Stella and her Gigi.

Copyright © 2024

The summer is finally here!

Time to grow vegetables, fruits, flowers, and herbs in Gigi's garden.

Gigi's garden was looking a little sad and needed some extra love.

But what could we do?

One rainy Sunday, Gigi and I read a story together.

"Long, rainy days remind me of the importance of patience," Gigi said.

"In the Bible, one group of God's people were called the Israelites. The Israelites were slaves and waited many years to go back home," Gigi said.

God told the Israelites to be patient and strong. He promised the Israelites that one day they would grow strong, just like a beautiful garden.

The Israelites prayed for many
years and asked for freedom.

They waited on God's promise.

Many years later, the Israelites were free!

"God sends us blessings today just as He did in the Bible," Gigi said, "When God gives us rain, He blesses the earth and all of the gardens."

We decided to put on our rain boots and collect rainwater!

The next week, Gigi and I used our rainwater to water our plants.

We picked some spinach,
beets, cucumbers, carrots,
and tomatoes to make a
yummy salad.

After we finished eating, we put our leftover vegetables in the big compost bin.

"What is compost?" I asked Gigi.

"Compost makes plants happy. It is a source of food for plants and helps them grow," Gigi said.

The next day I went back to Gigi's house to help her water and feed the plants. This sparked a brilliant idea.

"What if we ask people at church to bring food to compost? It can help our plants grow stronger this season!" I said to Gigi.

"That is a wonderful idea," Gigi said.

Gigi and I made posters asking the church to bring items such as banana peels, orange peels, and carrot tops.

Our friends at church loved bringing leftovers for Gigi's garden compost!

The next few months flew by! Fall came, and Gigi and I could not believe our eyes. The compost was helping our plants grow!

Before we knew it, Gigi's small backyard garden became a community garden.

Many friends visited and helped us.

At the end of the fall harvest, Gigi and I picked
our last apples and made a yummy pie.

Gigi and I decided we would host a few friends
in need of love and joy for a Thanksgiving meal.

30

At the Thanksgiving meal, I tried my best to smile big at each of our friends.

As Gigi and I handed out food I thought about the story of the Israelites.

"The friends we are helping need love like the Israelites," I said to Gigi. "I am happy we can bless them with this yummy food."

At the end of the meal, Gigi and I hugged and said goodbye.

As Gigi hugged me she whispered something in my ear, "Always remember to do all things out of love, just like God loves us."

COMPOST GUIDE

GREEN MATERIALS

GRASS CHOPPING

TEA BAGS

RICE & GRAINS

EGG SHELLS

FEATHERS

FRESH LEAVES

HAIR

SEAWEED

FRUIT & VEG

AIFAFA MEAL

FRESH FLOWERS

COFFEE GROUND & FILTERS

KITCHEN SCRAPS

BROWN MATERIALS

CORNCORBS & STALKS

PAPER

SAWDUST & WOODSHAVINGS

DRY LEAVES

STRAW

WOOD CHIPS

TWIGS

VEGETABLE STALKS

SOILED NAPKINS & PAPER PLATES

PEAT MOSS

DO NOT COMPOST

What does the word harvest mean in the Christian tradition?

From a practical standpoint, harvesting is the process of collecting plants or animals for food. The symbolic meaning of harvest in Scripture has two main ideas, God's provision for his people and His overall blessing. One may only be lucky enough to celebrate one plentiful harvest season a year, but we experience the spirit of harvest daily.

Who were the Israelites?*

In the story told by Isaiah, the Israelites were exiled from their holy land due to their rebellion against God. During this difficult season, Isaiah tells the Israelites that they should not stray or isolate from God, but trust and call out to Him in their suffering.

What is the reference verse used for the story of the Israelites?

"The Lord will always lead you. He will satisfy your needs in dry lands. He will give strength to your bones. You will be like a garden that has much water. You will be like a spring that never runs dry." (Isaiah 58:11)

 *Source: https://dailyverse.knowing-jesus.com/isaiah-58-11